Blue — Poems & Prose
Copyright © 2020 by Dylan Dimitri Dias

All rights reserved. No part of this publication may be reproduced in any manner without the prior written consent of the author except in the case of reprints or in the context of reviews.

dylan@dylandias.ca

Cover art by Paweł Czerwiński on Unsplash
Cover design by Dylan Dimitri Dias
Cervanttis Signature Script by Creatype Studio

Printed and bound in the USA

BLUE

— Poems & Prose —

For Korra & Nabeeha

Amber	*1*
Yume	*3*
Fukai Mori	*5*
Toronto	*7*
Starlight	*9*
3 Minutes (a letter)	*11*
Ten Thousand Years	*13*
Westing	*15*
Mist	*17*
Apparitions	*19-21*
Narrative	*23-25*
The East River	*27*
Loss	*29-31*
Unread	*33*
Fossil	*35*
Roses	*37*
Sera	*39*
The Trees	*41*

Amber

In the pockets of light that pool between the leaves of fragrant trees

And in the rustle of the wind that touches the sidewalk

And then the fence, and then the edge of my hair

Underneath clouds that gather like gossamer in the breadth of a living sky

And glazed in the coral and saffron of an early evening

I catch the scent of sweet Autumn

Like a veil draped loosely over the smoke of the city

Reminding me to not turn away

Asking me to look you in the eyes, the lips, the cheeks, and the nose

And imagine myself kissing you there

Connecting the deepest cracks in the earth

Illuminating the darkest depths of the ocean

And merging the widest tears in the atmosphere

I caught you, sunlight

In the subtle warmth of this moment

In the palm of his hand at my side

In the vibration of his skin against my own

In the gleam of his iris

The colour of sand at sunset

Piercing into me

Like a bullet

Asking me

To be here

To be his

Yume

How many more times can I look at my hand

Before its ridges become foreign

These palms

A linear graph of every childhood disappointment

Every adolescent disparity

Every adult longing

The secrets of me

The truth of me

Dried on the redness of my skin

Fukai Mori

Somewhere between spring and summer is loss

I'd rather take a hit than listen to that song one more time

I promised myself something greater, I'd think, in the tight bark of my skin

Though, I suppose, resilience is its own virtue

At night I think of times I should've been there

During the day I think of things I wish I'd said

I am reduced, every time, to the boy I've always been

My sweet man, I wonder where you've taken my life

Into the shining belly of the Kohaku, where purity sinks into the ocean

Into the deep earth of the Kodama, where austerity outlasts time

Or into the wreathed arms of Azna, where glory and death are one and the same

I am tired of being human

I am starving to be human

Toronto

If only I shared my bed that night with you

I'm sorry, I was still young

I was afraid of being too close, or more importantly, not fantastic enough

How could you possibly notice the bend in my neck

The way that I notice yours — I'd think

Or why would you wait for the sunrise to gloss just slightly across my arm

And then my chest

Before warming our bed — the way that I do

I'm not beautiful — I'd say to myself

The moonlight won't give me elegance

And before you walked in, before you even had a moment to speak

I already left you

Starlight

All I see is starlight
When I imagine you here
There's a lake, steady and glistening
Against the powder glow of the moon
An iris of lightning to break the clouds
Surrounding you in curtains of light

"I'm here."

I see the earth in your eyes
The colour of midnight
Its heaviness, like the ocean, holding me

"Leave with me."

There's a zephyr — a fragrance
A silk gust that wraps around me
Its impermanence — a reminder

"This place isn't real."

I am always trying to find my way
Between the deeply cut wood of the forest
Beneath the fragments of moonlight
A kaleidoscope
Laced into the leaves of old, silent trees
Watching me
Lose myself
Like you — a ghost
Both here and invisible
Like the earth — a shell
Both whole and cracked

"I can't find you."

And your eyes — like meteors
A laser that cuts the sky
Setting me on fire

"I love you."

Wait — don't leave
Wait — I'm dying
Wait — for me

3 Minutes

I hope you didn't think I was awkward. I told you I had to be on set that morning, and I told you I needed to go. And I did, but I could've waited a few more seconds — to get your number, to invite you for coffee, to honestly tell you how I felt, for once. I think we met at Dundas and I had a clean 3 minutes to work out the best version of myself before I left at Wellesley — it wasn't enough. The blitz of the train was slower than my words, I'm certain. But you looked good. You looked great. Onto bigger things and brighter places — that's cliché, but no less true. Studying abroad, collaborating with talented people, building your life. I remember how we used to talk about film, about art, about music. Your compassion was as impressive as your taste, and I never forgot that. I can't believe it'd been 5 years since I hugged you last. Your eyes were the same — midnight blue, like the earth. I could only be so lucky.

But I know it's not completely real. It's foggy glass, and I can only just barely make out the shape of your face. I know you never really read my message, though you were sweet to me anyways. I guess I can't really describe what it feels like to slowly fall for someone, but I didn't know until we said goodbye 5 years ago. I thought I'd never see you again, and I accepted that I could never be that person to you. And in my obvious youth, in the drying air of that day, I puffed my chest, pushed it away, and let it disappear.

But then there I was, standing outside your train, wondering where this feeling had been for so long. Maybe I was lonely, or maybe I didn't realize how deeply I cared about you. It doesn't matter, I just wanted to be honest. I wanted to write, but I can't write that. I wanted to call, but I'm afraid I'd put some awkward pressure on you. I needed it to come from you, but I know it won't. And that's ok — I'm not trying to destroy myself or anything. It just feels strange to find something you never lost, and then feel like you've lost it again. But it's familiar — I've never not been the boy in the rain. Though your warmth always found a way through. I wish I could hold onto that. I wish I could remember the crease of your smile forever, but each day it fades a little.

These words have no power, no gale, no pigment or fragment of sound. They float to the highest, emptiest peak to become stardust, to become fragrance. Without you, but with all of me.

I miss you.

Ten Thousand Years

There you are
I heard the wind change
And I can see your face, finally
Sweet friend, I knew you'd be here
I was waiting for your smile
I was waiting for your eyes
The ones that open ridges and valleys in my chest

In the storm of us
We have the stillness of the earth
As patient and present
As it was ten thousand years ago
Time didn't touch this part
It was always going to be here
My beautiful boy
With hair the colour of maple
With arms that could hold all of me
I wish you found me
I wish these words could trace
The analemma of the sun
Into something the sky could never lose
And in another ten thousand years
They'd say it was a comet
Cutting the atmosphere
Leaving a message you'd always find
In the silver of moonlight

Everything I've loved has crystallized
Into the sapphire of this moment
Into the space between your lips
A constellation of missed words

My prince, my boundless river
In the dust of winter
I will fade
As you brighten
And our story will fall apart
And our voices will never quite meet
And our hands will never quite touch
And the earth will move on, anyways

Westing

You're looking away, again.

It's after 7, and the buildings across the street are starting to flicker.
The wind against your back has caught the looseness of your collar, and the amber
of the evening has rested on the curve of your face.
And still, your eyes are elsewhere.

"Are you ok?"

Your lips are heavy.
I just want to kiss you.

"Mostly."

The slow temperance of dusk is settling into the air.
If I look away now, the breeze might carry you.
But I know you'd rather not be here.
I know the earth is tiring.

If you'd like me to, I'll join you,
And lay the roses out beneath your feet.

"Ask me to stay, and I will."

Being held by you is like going home.
I can feel the sun rising in the breath of your chest —
Warm, strong, compassionate, and old.
Pulling you, in fragments, to the west.

"Disappear with me."

The distant, stellar sky.
The last place to long for.
High above the fossil of living.
Inside the unrest of us.

Even with you — I disintegrate.

Mist

I've been listening to the wind lately
The way it lifts the canopy of the forest
Like blistered silk
Across the belly of the Earth
A shadow — like you
Like the coming of nightfall

There's always something to be heard
In the cosmic procession of starlight
Its glitter has rested on my skin
And I am sapphire
Precious, resting, waiting
For connections in the soil
For the polished oil of your sweat
To take hold of my neck
To dig cavities into my chest
To find the pieces of me I've lost in the sand

And the sequoias — like sentries to the sky
And their leaves — like clusters of silver
The pillars of my ascension
A merkabah of clay and dirt
On the crest of cracked lightning
Into the blue gossamer
Of midnight mist

Apparitions

"I needed you."
"I wasn't trying to hurt you."
"I know — it's not in your nature."
"But you're upset."
"I almost lost everything. There was so much emptiness. And the people I thought would be there — they weren't really there."
"I didn't know."
"Because you weren't there."
"I'm sorry."
"I felt like I was dying. I wish you told me."
"Would it have made a difference?"
"If we spoke — yes."
"And if we didn't?"
"I was always running home to myself. There was never anything there. I hated mornings for so long."
"I'm sorry I wasn't there to wake up with you."
"It's my destiny."
"Loneliness isn't a destiny."
"No — you're right. It's just my story."
"I'm with you now."
"Love is fickle."
"Do you love me?"
"I do — that's strange to say."
"Then let's start now."
"I'm not sure you even know me."
"Do you know me?"
"Why are you here?"
"To find something."

Apparitions

The earth could've been warmer that day
I often wrote letters about you when it snowed
And I'd find myself returning to the same parks and pathways under the viaduct

There was always something to reclaim in the bitterness of morning
There was always a memory I forgot to write down
I can't quite tell if you're real — my glasses are full of fog
But I can hear your voice cutting into the wind
It reaches me just barely

Is this an apparition

A cold whisper, the crisp edge of your words, resting on the curve of my right cheek
Something clever, something honest — that's so like you
I must be so sweet to remember you this way, still
I must be lost

A thousand letters won't change our distance
Somewhere between the Don and Riverdale
Somewhere between Dufferin and Cottingham

I became a ghost

Narrative

"Having someone there makes it easier."
"I found someone."
"I'm talking to a boy."
"Yeah, I'm just having fun."
"He's so sweet."
"He's texting me."
"It's easy with him."
"I don't feel like being alone right now."
"We just lied on the couch together."
"He asked me about what makes me happy."
"I met someone at a club."
"I met a boy."
"I like that he likes to rub my back."
"He's affectionate."
"We drove around all night."
"I like the way he touches my face."
"We talk all the time."
"We understand each other."
"He's gentle."
"He cares about me."

Narrative

"He doesn't like Asian dudes."
"He's not into femme and fat."
"He's married."
"I asked him what he wanted to do."
"I apologized before we met."
"He said I shouldn't really talk back to him."
"He said there's no way he'd ever be into me."
"I said I'm sorry about my body."
"He asked me to be discreet."
"He wants pics."
"I didn't hear back from him."
"He said to forget about him."
"They were staring at me like I shouldn't be there."
"He said he'd come over but that he wouldn't kiss me."
"He's expecting me to go all the way."
"He said he doesn't want to waste his time."
"I'm not going to try."
"He just wanted to experiment."
"I don't think he's interested."
"I'm pretty lonely."
"I'm not his type."
"I've never had a place here."
"He won't see me."
"He told me to keep my clothes on."
"I didn't want to take my clothes off."
"It's heartbreaking."
"It's normal."
"I'm tired."

The East River

Last night was rough, again

But the moonlight was still there

A blue echo that collects the valley

A silent vapour that holds the east river

The sound of midnight carves wells into my chest

A dry erosion — a reminder, like powder, lost to the wind

It was never quite a story — just a vacant youth

A hollow figure at the edge of the lake

A fragment of a place I've never been

A distance he never crossed

Loss

"Wait a minute — before you go. Can we talk?"
"Yeah, ok."
"Don't be upset. You mean a lot to me."
"I'm happy for you."
"I know. I just wanted to make sure you were ok."
"I'm not sure I am, but I didn't want to say that. You mean a lot to me too."
"You seemed distant tonight."
"It's been a long time. I haven't felt like this in years. I think you're wonderful — I'm just not very good at this."
"You always say things that aren't quite what you want to say."
"I know I'm obvious."
"Sometimes. I'm just worried about you."
"It sucks — losing people."
"You're not going to lose me."
"I already am."
"We'll stay close. I'll always write you, I promise. I'm not willing to lose everything we share together."
"It will change though."
"Why?"
"Because it will. These connections are beautiful — but then you don't see one another for coffee every week. You might not call so often like you used to, or send one another texts when you need someone to know that something's happened, finally. A week will pass, and then a month, and maybe a few more. It will disintegrate."
"Only if we allow it to. I can't imagine not speaking to you."
"It's not that simple. Maybe we'll FaceTime when we can. Maybe we'll still share stories. And when you visit — maybe we'll pick up where we left off and have a great time. But it won't be the same. The proximity of us, the feel of your heartbeat when I hug you, the scent of your neck — it will start to fade."
"I won't let it."
"It's not up to you. We can't bottle this moment."
"I'm losing you. Just stop — slow down."
"Nothing lasts."
"Why do you have to be so honest?"
"Why do you have to go?"
"I'm losing you."
"You are. I'm sorry."
"No — I'm sorry."

Loss

There's a crack in the earth and a tightness in my chest

Something's burning. I want to throw up. I need to get out of here

Memory is a gift, but it's full of shit

It's all blank, it's all unfinished

Somewhere in the ocean, somewhere between the clouds — I had a story

But I don't remember what I was supposed to say

I don't remember his name

Where did we eat lunch that day

What time was it when I stared back at his apartment window after I left

I think I was there for too long

Something was falling apart, something turned to liquid in my hands

All I remember is longing

All I have is effervescence

Unread

Loneliness stings

Every time

Even though

It's every day

Even though

I play the same music

Whenever I miss

Writing you

Whenever you don't

Respond

And I keep staring

At that send button

Like it's a bullet

I have to take

Just so you'd see

My words

And think of me

Again

Fossil

I'm sorry if I crumble
Wrapped in you
But I'm glad you made it, anyways
Because I wasn't thinking
And I had a bad attack again
And even though you said you couldn't
I'm glad you stayed
Even if it's just a minute longer
Even if it's just to remind me
That this is over
It feels so childish
To still need this
Your arms and the heat of your chest
Your hair and the colour of your skin
The teal of the evening
Resting on your shoulders
I'll pretend not to notice
That your eyes look darker than usual
Like polished obsidian
Like the vacuum of midnight
Pulling me closer
Tearing me apart
Like it's gravity
And not just
The way you look at me
I'll pretend that I'm ready
To loosen my grip
So that you know it's safe
To let go
And I'll pretend to walk away
Instead of sinking into the asphalt
A fossil on the street
That I'd hope
You'd never trip over
Again

Roses

Let me be clear
Because I know it's too sudden
And I know it's too raw
To feel his body get heavy
And I noticed you holding your head
In your hands
When the air got drier in the room
And the walls started to peel
Heroes leave holes
Carved into the earth
So that we can be lighter
When the dullness of night passes
Heroes leave roses
Where sand once was
So fragrant
That every morning without them
Is still familiar
And the depth of this
And the gravity that holds us
So low
Will dissolve with the newness
Of every season
So the sky can be closer
So the moon can be brighter
So we can see in the dark
And try again

Sera

"I just need you to tell me it's fine."

"It's fine, or it will be. And I'm here."

"I feel invisible."

"I'm holding you."

"Everything I build is fragile."

"Except this."

"I'm angry all the time."

"Because it matters to you."

"I'm tired."

"Because you've tried."

"I don't know what's next."

"It's wherever we are, together."

The Trees

I didn't see you there
I was listening to the trees
If you walk the Don before noon on a warm Sunday, all you hear are the trees
They bend and flutter as if you've arrived, finally, just to see them

I always feel alone here
It's just me, trying to be present, and hoping there's some energy that takes notice
But it's a silent companionship — the echo of nature
It isn't dead, but it's unconcerned with the humanness of you
I find it compelling, in a lonely way
The only magic here is the magic we choose to see
Maybe that's also life

I hope it's ok that I'm tired
I'm not honest to hurt people, but there's a cost for finding your authenticity
Sometimes it's not as bright as you wished it'd be
Sometimes the bits and pieces of love you come across aren't quite enough
The staleness of being outlasts everything — it's fire I'm searching for, not stone
But distance is a heavy mantle, like truth, unwavering and unmoving
If it's God carving our pathways into this earth
Then it's only her breath that can bend the mountains
I am seeking the last river home

But I am lost in a great kingdom
My dreams — they float above me and around me like vapour
Like a sheath of silk that barely holds the wind
Somewhere between the zephyr is your face, your skin — the scent of you
A glimmer of starlight in the bitter concrete
My feet hold onto the pavement as if it were about to evaporate

"Take me elsewhere."

I'm looking for air in the ocean, again
I'm an artist, not a hero
And this petition, this bonfire of adolescent hope, won't find you

People who have people say that I'll be ok
People building their futures say that mine is bright
People with privilege say that I'll get there
But it's all relative
Their stories are the missing pages from mine
And here I am, still searching

I still stare at the moon at night like it's a gateway to Andromeda
I still find the depth of the ocean as mysterious as midnight
And I still wait for spring to hear the tide of the trees
Gliding across the valley in Azna's morning yawn

I'm here

Lightning Source UK Ltd.
Milton Keynes UK
UKHW020135291220
375862UK00008B/1637